These People.

I0838868

What is this book about? Well, to be honest, the inspiration for this book came from George Bush Jr…or rather his followers…when they suddenly vanished from the face of the Earth when his Presidency ended.

I call this time… *The Great Disappearance.*

Yup, when Bush's term ended, it was like his followers vanished in a wisp of smoke. You couldn't find a Bush supporter after he left office. Hell, even after all these years its damn near impossible to find a Republican who will admit to voting for Bush.

It never happened…somehow the man won two terms without a single voter.

It's even worse now…now that Trump has poisoned the Republican party…far worse.

Now, before we do this, I want to explain things a bit.

First, I want you all to know that I grew up redneck, redneck as hell, in Citrus County Florida. I grew up shooting guns, going to biker parties, (I didn't think about the fact that they were bikers, being so young, but that's what they were, my friends' parents, bikers.) I spent my days fishing, atv riding, running in cow fields, and going to flea markets every weekend. I lived the redneck experience when I was young, I really did, and it wasn't bad. To me, back then, being a conservative meant keeping things simple, enjoying what you had, and protecting the wilderness and wildlife that lived in it.

That's what it meant to me.

However, even then, back when I was a kid, I knew there was an extreme version of this life…the freaks, not that I called them that at the time, I simply avoided these people…the racists, the haters, the dumb dumbs…the true rednecks. All I wanted from these people was distance. Even then I knew these people should never be put in charge of anything, that they were different than the rest. These were the people who couldn't have a conversation without using the word nigger. These were the people wearing the Nazi and confederate tattoos on their arms, proudly displaying the flags of hate over their trailers, on the back of their trucks…but claiming to somehow be proud Americans.

But it really didn't matter to me…not back then…they were just a joke, what we kids swore we would never be.

Oh, how times have changed.

These people, consumed by hate, unable to differentiate between what would have once been on the cover of a supermarket tabloid and the real news, now have a voice…a hate monster, a man just as racist as them and fueled by the isolation that comes with being rich and out of touch, and just as confused by the reality of life and the horseshit the internet spreads as they are.

Trump.

Never has there been a case in American history so ridiculous as the one we now face, when the dirt-poor worship a criminal conman, some even placing him above Jesus himself. They flock to the poles in numbers never seen before, all desperate to cast their vote for a man who wouldn't piss on their face if they were on fire. I see these people every day, hour after hour, as I work the world of retail. They are easy to spot…they stand out like a black cloud in a clear blue sky. How? It's the hate, it consumes them, creates an aura around them they can't escape…it's the pure hate in their eyes.

All I wish to accomplish with this short book is to create a written time capsule for future generations to see…of a time when hate consumed, and Jesus was kicked to the side by Christians in favor of a man who has spent every day of his life in complete opposition to their sacred 10 commandments.

Seriously…what part of this list is Trump?

The Ten Commandments. (Some of you Christians out there have never read this.)

1   "I am the Lord your God, who brought you out of the land of Egypt, out of the house of bondage. You shall have no other gods before Me.

2   "You shall not make for yourself a carved image, or any likeness of anything

that is in heaven above, or that is in the earth beneath, or that is in the water under the earth; you shall not bow down to them nor serve them. For I, the Lord your God, am a jealous God, visiting the iniquity of the fathers on the children to the third and fourth generations of those who hate Me, but showing mercy to thousands, to those who love Me and keep My Commandments.

3	"You shall not take the name of the Lord your God in vain, for the Lord will not hold him guiltless who takes His name in vain.

4	"Remember the Sabbath day, to keep it holy. Six days you shall labor and do all your work, but the seventh day is the Sabbath of the Lord your God. In it you shall do no work: you, nor your son, nor your daughter, nor your male servant, nor your female servant, nor your cattle, nor your stranger who is within your gates. For in six days the Lord made the heavens and the earth, the sea, and all that is in them, and rested the seventh day. Therefore the Lord blessed the Sabbath day and hallowed it.

5	"Honor your father and your mother, that your days may be long upon the land which the Lord your God is giving you.

6	"You shall not murder.

7	"You shall not commit adultery.

8	"You shall not steal.

9	"You shall not bear false witness against your neighbor.

10	"You shall not covet your neighbor's house; you shall not covet your neighbor's wife, nor his male servant, nor his female servant, nor his ox, nor his donkey, nor anything that is your neighbor's."

 Honestly…people think Trump was sent by god…can you read any of that, any of it, and say Trump is in line with it…of course not.

But let's see what Jesus says…and how it fits Trump a little more.

Jesus: "Those who exalt themselves will be humbled, and those who humble themselves will be exalted."

Trump: "Sorry losers and haters, but my I.Q. is one of the highest -- and you all know it! Please don't feel so stupid or insecure, it's not your fault."

Jesus: "I have not come to call the righteous, but sinners to repentance."

Trump: "Why do I have to repent, why do I have to ask for forgiveness if [I'm] not making mistakes?"

Jesus: "Blessed are the meek, for they shall inherit the earth."

Trump: "I fully think apologizing is a great thing. But you have to be WRONG … I will absolutely apologize sometime in the hopefully distant future if I'm ever wrong."

Jesus: "Blessed are the peacemakers, for they will be called children of God."

Trump: "I could stand in the middle of Fifth Avenue and shoot somebody and I wouldn't lose voters."

Jesus: "Do not store up for yourselves treasures on earth, where moths and vermin destroy, and where thieves break in and steal. But store up for yourselves treasures in heaven, where moths and vermin do not destroy, and where thieves do not break in and steal. For where your treasure is, there your heart will be also."

Trump: "Part of the beauty of me is that I'm very rich."

Jesus: "This is my body which is given for you; do this in remembrance of me. …This cup is the new covenant in my blood, which is poured out for you."

Trump: "When I go to church and when I drink my little wine and have my little cracker, I guess that is a form of forgiveness. I do that as often as I can because I feel cleansed."

Jesus: "Love your enemies, do good to those who hate you, bless those who curse you."

Trump: "When people wrong you, go after those people, because it is a good feeling and because other people will see you doing it. I always get even."

In truth, all religion is to Trump…is another scam. However, for most Christians, including most of the ones I grew up with, that's all it was to them as well. I mean seriously, have you ever driven by a church on Sunday and looked at the 20-25 cars parked there and thought to yourself, shit, is that really all the people who go to church? Granted, there are thousands of churches, and each has its own collection cult of eager cracker eaters, but still…the numbers are always low, far lower than they should be for them to have such power over the country…the world.

And all Trump has to do to win these people over is say…I'm one of you…and he's in…it's fucking crazy.

But what's even more crazy is the fact that Joe Biden is the religious goody goody, a lifetime cracker eater…and they hate him. How does that make sense?

Now that doesn't mean I'm a Biden supporter, not really, but I honestly would have voted for roadkill if it were up against Trump…so Biden was my guy.

And no matter who the next President is, no matter who the next 5-6 Presidents are, they will be stuck fixing the fucking mess Trump created.

So, what's this book about….?

Well, it's simple. I just want to point out how truly lost these people are…how blind they were to the past 4 years of Trump's criminal Presidency….so in time, when the terrible realities of it do finally sink in…they can't just hide away, blend into the background like Bush Jr followers did.

Am I defending Biden…no, not really, some of the things he has done haven't been very good….but seriously, when you toss a match into a dumpster and walk away laughing, you don't suddenly jump out when the fire department shows up and blame them for starting the fire.

Anyway, all I want to do is show some truly innocent posts made by President Joe Biden and the Republican reaction to them...because it's truly disgusting, and very frightening that even after his defeat...how truly brainwashed Trumps' cult followers still are.

**Side note...I may chime in from time to time with a response to various posts. I have also left the posts, as* *is, as I feel it plays into who these people are. These are their real posts.*

 **Emojis have been removed...not by choice, but due to the fact they were not supported when attempting to print book. Believe me, I think silly little pictures are very much a Trump thing...I simply couldn't get them through.*

 Let's begin...

<u>Joe Biden</u>

"The United States will ban Russian-affiliated ships from our ports.

That means no ship that sails under the Russian flag or that is owned or operated by a Russian interest will be allowed to dock in a United States port or access our shores. None.

(Obviously this is in response to Russia invading Ukraine…you know, the country Trump tried to blackmail in exchange for information on Biden's son when they came to him for help against the growing threat of Russian hostility.)

Regina S.

This is the last place they would want to come to. You have trashed this country!

(Remember this post…)

Kenny P.

Can we ban you Joe

Vijaykumar H.

It is our responsibility to defend our southern border and the Wall built by spending plenty of American money.

(Fake account. Trying to preach Trump shit. You will see many fake accounts, which I found surprising…but not really, not if you really think about it.)

Rita M.

Who cares what your opinion is?

*(*Answer- The World.)*

Barbara L.

Destroying America every single way they can. Hope you're all very pleased with this destructive administration.

(Just angry hate.)

Were B.

What a rediculous decision

(Why? Please explain....at least use spell check first. Ridiculous > Rediculous.)

Jeff B.

You do know a huge amount of agricultural fertilizer that we need to grow food comes on those ships? Do you have a plan for that, or are you going to tell us we'll just have to live with higher food prices? Or just blame it on Putin?

(This guy thinks America can't produce enough shit.)

Daryl H.

Awww someone got their wittle feelings hurt. Joe this dose nothing for America

(Not meant to do anything for America.)

Pedro M.

Which flag are going to have ships which bring the uranium US purchases to Russia?

(I guess this is tapping into debunked conspiracy nonsense Trump and his lot tried to push in 2016.)

Freedom J. C.

Who needs your ports when your economy scrambling under the feet of USSR???

*(*Fake Account- supporting Russia.*)*

Marial M. A.

Funding war mr. President Joe biden

(Your guess is as good as mine on this one. I guess she is angry because we are supporting the Ukraine, meaning she supports Russia?*)*

Joshua M. S.

You Democrats are amazing. Lol

(How so...? What would this guy do?)

Prince I.

So you can't beat Russia huh? Mr sanctions all the way

(Pure Pro-Russian support. Do you really think this guy knows what's going on?)

Christopher M.

Bad President with bad heart

(What do you think he thought about Trump?)

Biblop H. A.

Really so funny man president joe biden

(Fake account.)

Hon M. M. S.

You're too soft to lead the nation

You're too soft to lead the world. Sometimes you make me miss Donald Trump. Why doesn't America intervene militarily to save Ukraine, or is it that you are afraid of Russians? Ukraine is the second Afghanistan 🇦🇫 for Russia 🇷🇺

(Obviously a post from a non-American trying at first to sound American...preaching war, Pro-Russia, Pro-Trump...Fake account.)

Norberto F.

Worst president of our time.

(Obviously a Pro-Trumper trying to somehow make people forget about the last 4 years of Trumpism. Possibly a fake account.)

Brian F.

Let's go Brandon

(Speaks for itself. All the average Republican can come up with.)

Jim K.

Do you think that will stop them Joe Biden ? Your sanctions are weak and ineffective. If you really wanted to get tough you should have never allowed back door payoffs through your son Hunter.

(Fox news Republican here.)

Tina M. D.

Democrats ..."TAX THE RICH! CORPORATIONS ARE EVIL AND NEED TO PAY THEIR FAIR SHARE! Well, except for Disney."

(Florida Republican preaching the nonsense of their Governor.)

Donald C.C.B

I wish you had the same laws for the southern borders LOL when it comes to immigration

(Southern border craziness.)

Deb B.

Try banning terrorists, gangs, drug traffickers, & human trafficking on our OWN southern border! You know the thing….protecting the nation & its citizens your job.

(All those things have been banned forever. Pure Trumpism with this one.)

?

This is the last place they would want to come to. You have trashed this country!

(Sound familiar? Remember the first post I suggested you remember? This account was so fake that my computer couldn't even translate the name.)

Theresa P.

North Dakota is considering legislation that would require the state to examine every executive order signed by biden (he does not deserve the respect of capitalizing his name) to determine its constitutionality, potentially nullifying the majority of bidens decrees within the state.

(Pure craziness. What the hell is she even talking about? I doubt she even knows.)

Chase H.

That will really help with food and supply shortages. Inflation and all.

They know what they are doing people.

(Pro-Russia. I guess he thinks a President can only do 1 thing at a time.)

Chris F.

Are you going to give back the kickback money you got from Russia?

(Pure Trumpism.)

Mirella L.

Oh I am sure you will care about that there is a nuclear war with Russia.. Joe Biden ...

(Huh? Is this lady actually wanting a war? Pro-Russia.)

Uzoma N.

Sleeping Joe, USA is gone on your watch.

(Fake account. Trumpism.)

Nick P.

Why do Covid rates keep going up as the number of people vaccinated do?

(No clue...must have seen something on his favorite conspiracy page. Unless he is speaking of Omicron...but even then, he would be wrong.)

Dave L.N.

Let's go Brandon

Chlamy G.

LETS GO BRANDON

Tom S.

hey braindead joe why are you supporting nazi in Ukraine??

Vladimir Putin: The world today calls me a murderer because I protect my people and my country. Russia is not at war with the Ukrainian citizens but against Nazis. are soldiers are doing everything they can to protect the Ukrainian residents. And if the West accuses me of defending my brothers and compatriots I have no words.

(Obviously a nut-job. Pro-Russia. Fake account.)

Michelle S.B.

GET OUT OF OUR WHITE HOUSE AUTHUR ROBERTS AKA BIDEN .....

(Conspiracy craziness. Pro-Trump.)

Donna K.

That's telling em. Way to hurt your fellow man. You actually think hurting the Russian citizens is going to stop Putin? Mean tweets, cheap gas, world peace. Trump 2024!

(Wow, what really needs said? Pro-Russia, Pro-Trump, pure crazy

David C.

I see that you are getting bribes from other countries to do this

(Got any proof...? Just Republican conspiracy shit.)

Herman C. B.

Joe you had time head this problem off a year ago. You meet with Putin and could have fixed this but as usual you were scared of him and did nothing. A year ago you could have put a 100 thousand troops in Ukraine and Russia would not have dared invade them. You are responsible but never take responsibility but as usual want to blame others for your failure. That's the democrats way.

(What do you think this guy thought about Trump doing absolutely nothing about Putin for 4 years? What do you think he would have said if Biden did send troops into Ukraine? Pure Trumper.)

David C.

At the end of the day ole shit pants Joe shit in his pants

Paul X B.

youre caught up in war while you failed to deliver proper policies to your own people. you are a failure.

 (Fake account. You think this guy really knows what's going on? You think he understands Republican obstruction?)

Louie K.

Gee you Dolt, why didn't you do this a year ago when he was lining the border with his soldiers?

(Again, what do you think this guy thought about Trump doing nothing about Russia as it planned this? What do you think he thought about Trump trying to blackmail Ukraine?)

---}

Joe Biden

We must protect the air we breathe, the water we

drink, and treasured wildlife by advancing ambitious plans to protect our climate.

Our clean energy plan will create good-paying union jobs, lower costs, and improve the health and security of communities across America.

*Protecting the planet...no way Republicans have an issue with this...right?

<u>WRONG!!!!!</u>

*Side note- A Texas National Guard member, Spc. Bishop Evans, who drowned on the U.S.-Mexico border while on duty, was attempting to help a migrants who were struggling to swim across, state officials said Wednesday.

(WATCH HOW THEY USE THIS AGAINST BIDEN...EVEN THOUGH HE WAS NOT THE ONE TO SEND THE NATIONAL GUARD TO THE BORDER.)

Carmen S.

Let's go to the grand canyon so the background is a distraction and they don't notice the mumbling.. great job WH coordinators. you really know about placement

Andy C.

Here's an idea, let's resume importing oil from countries with no environmental regulations and then ship that dirty oil on cargo ships that burn fossil fuels across the whole freaking ocean also endangering the environment at the same time.

Global warming or whatever it's called these days is nothing but a money making machine and a way to brainwash supporters

Vijaykumar H.

We must protect the southern border and Wall. It is our duty as true American.

(From India.)

Don H.

We all love your runnaway inflation. I see it everyday and it effects every American. Im sure everyone loves having less in all aspects of their lives.

Clint S.

Oddly enough he's at the Grand Canyon. The pollution that makes it hazy to look across the entire canyon is from a Democrat controlled state and city of Los Angeles. The rangers have a station that monitor it.

Gretchen P.

And pollute the soil. NICE EXCHANGE.

Kerry J.

What about the border patrol! Where's their support

Stanley S.

The United States already does all those things. Quit the power grab.

Jennifer K.

You should be protecting our Southern border!

Chris H.

Thank you Big Guy!

I remember when you were a National Park Ranger at Jelly Stone Park. You did a great job keeping Yogi away from the picanick baskets.

Sandy T. B.

You must protect our borders !!!!

Race T.

Would be terrible if he stumbled of the edge of the Grand Canyon.....

Jan A. B.

Look away from the dumpster fire of: trafficking, drug smuggling, gas prices, inflation, open borders with unvetted criminals coming into our country, no prosecution of career criminals, purchasing oil from countries who don't care about the environment and killing our energy independence? No problem.

Brooke B. L.

Your laws and bills are never what they seem. You include whatever flavor of the week agenda is floating around DC and promote. You stand for nothing

Kathe M. M.

Everyone needs a good paying job, not just those who belong to a union. Unions donate heavily to Democrats so one hand washes the other. Despicable!

Cindy J. K.

Biden is anti American. He is showing his true colors by leaving our birder wide open without a plan in place. The states that receive his middle of the moght flights should immediately send these illegals to DC, Delaware, and wherever else these Democrats reside. Place officers at the airports to intercept these flight. Show Biden your state is not behind his invasion of illegals into our country. He aiding the cartels!

Scott M.

Broken record at it again, meanwhile inflation is at a 40 year high, gas prices are skyrocketing and you really have no idea what's going on!

Shirley S.

How about protecting our citizens??? Your open borders are hurting and killing Americans and you still don't care!

Billy R.

How about protecting the American people from the invasion at the Southern boarder. Unvetted criminals and terrorists crossing the boarder and causing crime, and chaos.

Steven M.

Today is Saturday April 23 2022 & Joe Biden is still the worst President we have ever had.

(A cut and paste champion here.)

Ginny C. J.

Let's ignore all the other problems like immigration, defunding the police, inflation. You really don't care about the important issues.

James S.

And y'all seriously believe this is Biden's Facebook page? He can't complete a sentence without mumbling and losing track of what he's saying. Do you really believe he would be on Facebook? Gullible Democrats!

Joanne B.

And send the entire nation into inflationary recession because of poor planning!

Michelle M. R.

What about protecting our borders??? The TX National Guard soldier who drowned today?? That's on you!

Tim J.

At what cost to the average American? Another Biden failure. The list continues to grow. Clown, clown, clown.

(Another Biden failure...you think he could at least give this a day before saying something?)

Jerry D.

What are you doing in Delaware again? Wasn't long ago all I heard was trumps golfing! 28% of your presidency is spent in Delaware! Are you getting health treatments? I won't ask other possibilities it could be! Please step aside! Let's find someone else capable and not Harris!

Debra B.

How about PROTECT OUR BIRDERS. You want to protect things? Start at the border!!!!!!!

John S.

Why don't you donate your salary to the cause.

Celia H.

Wonder how much they paid them people to sit there and make like they were listening to him!!!

Richard M.

Let's go Brandon !!! Where's all that money Joe !? Tell us about it Big Guy !!! Counting the seconds till your out of office Sooner is better than later … Impeach !!! Angry face, puke.

(Can you feel the blind hate?)

Pam P.

Joe we must protect ourselves from you! Everything you touch goes very badly!

Mick C.

And further put our country into debt with the pork you add to every bill.

Gerardo Z.

If your build back better plan is just like your first year in office We don't want it !!!

LETS GO BRANDON all the way !!!!

Regina P.

My Father created your mother bare shelves biden and He will handle what He created!

(Religious nut.)

Jeremy L.

So stop giving a billion dollars to the meat industry to destroy our planet

Gennan C. C.

You've done nothing but destroy this country since becoming PINO.

?

The only things that are urgent are sealing the Southern border and stopping inflation!

(Lives in Africa.)

Brent C.

Whatever you can't even protect the border..FJB

(Lives in Kentucky...complaining about the border.)

Augie B.

Of course Union jobs, and screw everyone else.

Ann S.

Close our borders to drug cartels incompetent Joe!!!!

Richard P.

Just do America a favor and turn around and keep walking!

Steve H.

So are why are you launching 100% more Rockets then you did in the 80s and there's only supposably one station?

Ishimo B.

I always burn some tires for earth day and this year I spray painted crazy China joe on them to honor our illegal president.

Keith C.

The Master of Spin has spoken again. Let's go, Brandon!

Joe E.

Why is it always union jobs? Why not just jobs?!?!

Ellen G. L.

We must protect America from the likes of you and the democrats that are destroying our country.

Patricia M.

Worse president in history

Roger H.

Can't protect the air if you can't protect the border?

Jennifer R.

Everyday I count down the days until you are never in office again. Biden's America sucks and democrats will learn they are not what American's want. Biden sucks

Dawn Z.

The problem is you and your family are breathing our air

Joe S

Generically-worded garbage.

David O.

LET'S GO BRANDON!!!

Rath B.

Standing in front of another screen. Lol

Nancita L.

Who's that guy at the podium?

Grs S.

hey joe go to Russsia, China, North Korea and Iran to give your clean energy speech - maybe they will listen to you! Lets go Branden

Daryl C.

How about Protecting our Border? We lost a life today trying to save an illegal migrant coming over the border this afternoon

Mary B. B.

You now have a death on your hands now since the soldier is presumed drowned due to you not closing the border! We don't want these people coming over! Do you not get this??? We are sick of your lame policies!

Andrea W.

What are you doing about the boarder and our man we just lost trying to save a illegal?

Lorisa C.

Sounds like Obama talking through his earpiece!

Cory K.

You cannot even fix our everyday problems, do you think that we are stupid enough to think that we should trust you with trillions to save the planet?

Diane B.

Because of your failure to secure the southern border, you are responsible for the death of a US citizen at the border who was helping to do the job the federal government is responsible for. You are a total FAILURE!!!?

Pam S.

Another death on your hands. You and the illegal immigrant should both be charged in the death of the Texas guardsmen

William A. S. Y.

If you really cared about Americans "security" you'd close the open

borders . Big Guy

Dale W. S.

The Wildlife Society Bulletin found that wind turbines killed an estimated 573,000 birds annually in the United States.

Marcel M.

What about the border?

The real "dreamers" are all the US citizens that wish our borders and immigration laws were enforced.

(Ohio.)

Pat M.

Everything.... And I mean EVERYTHING that you touch turns to absolute shit

John S.

Lots of words joy but most all of that is propaganda. Of course we all like clean water and air and, we have the cleanest in water and air in the world. Just more virtue signaling.

Kim O.

What about our BORDERS? What about inflation?

Bob R.

...ier it is destroying our country and his green deal has yet to create any jobs

Patrick S.

The Big Guy is only concerned about how to milk government programs to his own personal benefit. He could care less about anything else - especially the earth.

Dale W. S.

The Altamont Wind Resource Area in northern California alone killed over 2,000 Golden Eagles ...

Gary B.

Joe you gonna bring America back to the Stone Age

Louis O.

When will you visit our border and do something positive?

Brando L.

Nothing but more empty platitudes from a career politician.

All the Democrat Machine wants is yet more of your money to distribute to their faithful donors.

Wake the hell up!

Charlene Wiley

And what have you contributed aside from tons of carbon pollution with your jetting around everywhere?

Michael Darling

First, we must protect America from the Biden family.

Dave Maire

So what's your plan horse and buggy! Looks like your barking up the wrong tree the Amish already does that stupid!

Brian Fitch

Your plans always fail Brandon 􀀀

Bob Becker

This guy never says how he's going to save the country. All talk & no action. Full of wind!

John Schene

Your clean energy plan is killing the U.S. economy

 Brian Scott Foster

Stop the invasion on the southern border

*Ok, that's enough. There were still over 200 more comments, but you get the idea. Pure crazy Republican rage over Biden wanting to protect the environment.

  The guardsman they mentioned gave his life in an effort to save a human… These people sound like he was murdered or died trying to save a dog.

  (Yahoo News.) Via- Jason Duaine Hahn

Fri, April 22,

 A Texas Army National Guard soldier went missing along a river near the border of Mexico on Friday, the Texas National Guard said in a statement to PEOPLE.

The soldier had been assigned to Operation Lone Star, a border security initiative created by Texas Gov. Greg Abbott, the Texas Military Department said.

"A Texas Army National Guard Soldier assigned to Operation Lone Star has gone missing along the river during a mission-related incident, Friday April 22, 2022 in Eagle Pass, Texas," the Texas Military Department said.

*He died trying to save a human...

Joe Biden ·

Congratulations, Ketanji Brown Jackson.

Simply congratulating the newest Supreme Court appointee. This coming after Republicans blocked an Obama Appointee, supported an (alleged,) drunken rapist, then said nothing as Trump appointed (arguably,) the most unqualified woman to ever sit on the court. Do you think they might just accept her as a highly qualified judge, you know, after the shit they had pulled with the previous 2?

NOPE!!!!

Spaz

The only thing that is confirmed is your declining cognitive skills

(Do you think a guy calling himself Spaz is qualified to speak of mental health?)

Darlene Dubreuil Teddick Tedesco

I wonder how all the mom's feel about all the children that where abused and she gave all their abusers soft ball sentences ....yep she is a great judge.. and all you people that gave her all these sappy congratulations are not for our children ...shame on you all ..

Richard Sellers

Great another baby killer on the Supreme court.

Barbara Ralph

*History will remember this day because of the tilted playing field circumstances in which she got the position. She will always be the Supreme Court Justice with an *!*

Hunter Epperson

I guess none of these people listened to what her answers were and the way she side steped virtually every question. A sad day for America .

Jeffrey Stout

She had to make sure she used the words black women she should just be happy she got the position will it ever end why do we have to identify by race

Kim Piatkowski

Soft on criminals, pedophiles, as long as it's not her children or grandchildren, guess molesting little boys and girls are ok with all of you so happy to see her confirmed.

Lori Miller Lueder

To be nominated to such a position in these United States based solely on gender and skin color without much consideration of current and past judgements on cases presented before them, I would not be impressed with myself, and I doubt I would accept the position as a Justice of the United States Supreme Court. There are so many women of color whose judgements and backgrounds far exceed that of this particular female that would have done the position such good! RBG identifier she is NOT and will never hold a candle to.

Corrine Hagstrom Mosburg

So we are supposed to be proud of the fact that you nominated her because she is a woman but she doesn't actually know what a woman is?? We should feel like we are in good hands?? This administration is not working for the people of America.

Shane Borgman

Everyday that Joe Biden is President is bad for the American people. This woman only got her job because the color of her skin. She is not qualified for this job and the true American patriots know it!!

Scotty Smols

Affirmative action alive and well in the United States. Way to walk us backwards. You already picked the worst VP in history, thought you would have learned your lesson.

Maureen Yegge

This is a lifetime appointment, she is as far left as you can get, an Obama appointee, what is hell is wrong with people, why didn't they stop it! She is young, she will be in there spreading her crap for years to come. Obama is grinning happy as a clam, everything is going his way.

Jerald Belew

the only reason she was selected is because of her race and gender, no quality or merit

Tim DuMars

If she was the same woman only white she would never have gotten appointed. She is a weak liberal and we all know it and now get to watch as our country spirals more down the toilet. Thank you Mr Biden for all your not doing for our country!!! Amen

Tina Falkowski-Wirths

Oh yes, lets celebrate putting someone in the supreme court who was picked by skin color and gender. Not qualifications.

Good job.

And let's not forget bumbling Biden who once again embarrassed himself and our country.

Mark Greenwell

She was given this appointment because of her race,how embarrassing! Brandon is just pandering to his base. Heaven help us.

Nancy Miller

Biden live through his teeth as usual first of all she's number 115 not 200 next she did not go through nearly as much as Brett Kavanaugh dead that was the most despicable time of our country

Debbie Muirhead

I'm sure we'll remember once she starts voting everything far left when she gets in. She'll be so radical I'm sure there will be no way to forget her.

Sonia Lea

Affirmative Action has been around for a long time. It's sad that you got your job and so did KH based solely on your gender (though I know you don't know what that is) and the melanin in/of your skin. Next time, let's see people accomplish things based on their abilities. It's happened before!

Barb Tucker

Don't know what is the big deal as SHE stated she doesn't know what a woman is. Just another demorat publicity stunt to further destroy America.

It would be a shame if one of her daughters/granddaughters were sexually assaulted. Let's see how she would prosecute that offender.

Mary Cullum

Diamond & Silk should have been nominated & approved, they would have done some GREAT things for America, when a country turns it back on God & His values, this is what you get, common sense is not so common is it

Cheryl Pollock

Just because she is black doesn't mean she is good for the Supreme Court.

Carol Larry Breed

That fact is, If A Candidate for the Supreme Court Was Not A BLACK FEMALE, They were disqualified because if RACE and GENDER Even if they were more Qualified.

She is Certainly Qualified but, Nominated in a Very Racist Way.

Laura Carpenter

This is an example of racism. President Biden specifying the position will be filled by a black women. What about filling the position with the most qualified person, black, white, hispanic, etc.

This woman is a far left advocate whom doesn't know the definition of a woman. Come on man.....

Beverly Murphy

History ?? We'll if you want to say a Judge who doesn't follow the law well , you might have a point there !!!

Dolores Romano Downey

God please help our country because this "woman" who doesn't know what a woman is, will only hurt us

Kenneth William Lewis

Apparently the prerequisite was to be a judge who is a black woman. I wonder how many other Hispanic or other nationalities were over looked who could have been more qualified then this lady who couldn't even define what a woman is

Angela Cooke

Her position is more than humiliating since you made the world aware that you would be picking someone ONLY based on their GENDER and the COLOR of their skin.

John Eidson

.... and sleepy joe was the first man to threaten to with hold confirmation of a black woman nominated by President Bush and was successful in doing so. Just not his kind I guess.

Regina Cronan

And she actually thinks the whole country is applauding this. We know it is just a token What I don't understand is how the black people like her are so concerned with their heritage dand past but they marry white people. If it so important why do they not marry someone who shares the same heritage?

Betty Collins Mckinney

Well I'm thinking it's just a matter of time Gods gonna step in and say enough is enough the way this country is headed with all this crooked mess and this woman can't tell you what a woman is does not need to be in that position!!!!This ought to tell something!!!

Mark Moffett Jr

Way to discriminate, and openly admit you chose appoint someone based on race and not on really any other criteria. She may or may not be a balanced judge (granted not a good track record), but it loses all value, because you openly stated that you chose her because she was black.

Janis Richie

by her own word and science...she is NOT a woman!!! Arghhhhh

Matt Weisgerber

She will try people under military jurisdiction and we won't have a choice. She is not an interpreter of the constitution!

Carolyn Bourdeau

What gets me is that the Democrats made a big deal out of how the Republicans questioned her during the hearings. They are hoping nobody will remember how brutal they were to Judge Kavanaugh. That was horrible!

Shirley Michael

She only got the job because she is black !!! Not because she has the best qualifications! Pray for the Supreme Court, they will need it!

Marco Robof

So you have a Black woman at the supreme court but you really can't tell that because you (people) are not biologists. So it's useless to celebrate.. yeyyyy

Brent Lee

Sad indeed pick a judge by the color of her skin & not who is qualified

Judy Chambos

It's a shame that qualifications necessary were skin color and being a woman, something she doesn't want to give definition of.

Jacob Charlton

We certainly will remember... the day a woman selected to be in the most important position of legal power to translate and enforce constitutional law, sometimes dealing with "women's rights", couldn't define what a woman is... ▢

Barf

James Collier

But she can't define a woman when asked to during the confirmation process, so why is it so important that a black woman has been confirmed, LET THAT SET IN

Darlene Dubreuil Teddick Tedesco

This woman has hidden agenda..She is dangerous..You have to be if you give soft deals to child abusers...So I would not congratulation her.

Danny Osa Stanley

WE WILL REGRET THIS THE REST OF HER LIFE.

Sheila Blem

If she has socialist leanings like it was reported it's one more chunk out of our country and our freedom I wonder how many more of our government has socialist ties you know that is how they said they would conquer America is from within without a shot. WAKE UP SHEEPLE our country and freedoms are slipping away stop the madness

Wayne Day

History will certainly remember the day the Senate approved a very unqualified justice

Ginger Mellinger

▢ that women's idea of justice does not belong on the Supreme Court .... criminals have more rights than the victims in her mind... ... which is so wrong ..▢

Alan Loeffler

A woman who can't or won't define what a woman is. She also denies that mankind has innate rights given to us by a Creator. That means that she believe all rights are bestowed to us by the government. Sounds like an anti-constitutionalist to me!

***That was less than half the comments...but you get the idea.**

--}

Joe Biden ·

Today, we enshrine in law our recognition that the Postal Service is fundamental to our

economy, to our democracy, to our health, and the very sense of who we are as a nation.

Spaz

Yes .. Joe's the Postal Service great just like our inflation economy and our socialist democracy

DanDenise Mica

So glad to see the Governor of Texas stand against one of many bad policies By this President Hopefully other Governors will do the same

Jeremiah Kross

Only someone who spent their entire career living off the taxpayer dime

would consider the postal service a successful part of our economy. 🤣🤣

Mark Cook

How about you put the same effort into our borders!!!

(Lives in Maryland.)

Lisa Oliver Bennett

Exempt from the vaccine mandate which makes no sense.

□□□□ □□□

The affordable act which isn't affordable, destroyed our health care....health care went through the roof for us that pay and no longer can afford.

Carole Logue Buczek

Close the southern border! Thank you Governor Abbott all these illegals are heading to DC on the steps on the capitol maybe then you will do something you are the worst president ever

John Marron

You keep wanting to spend more of our money that we do not have. You have driven the value of the dollar down further every day so everything costs more money to buy!! You only support the rich entitled liberal elites and never do anything good for Americans!! Just quit!!

Tommy Wildermuth

You have surpassed Jimmy Carter as the worst POTUS in American history. Thank you

Catherine Kambua

USA has reduced herself to start fighting ladies... Sanctioning Putin 's daughter is cowardly act......go for men

Glory to Russia

Kimberly Mills

Hey joe, how did it feel to be completely ignored by everyone and to have obama turn his back on you when you called out his name and touched his shoulder to get included? Not even your own party wants anything to do with you. Very sad, but very fitting.

Daniel First

Wow. What a pressing matter when our economy is in absolute shambles...

Jason Mcgee

Close our borders!!!!!

Kelly Baker

joe you tanked our economy and your I said your oil policies

Paige Dunham

We know. Fair and honest elections are

HISTORY in the UNITED STATES OF AMERICA.

Johnny Cabrera

You mean the Postal Service that was Spying on Americans?

Brian Leonard

Why do Democrats insist on telling us who we are as a country? The last thing we need is a bunch of out of touch "elites" telling us who we are.

Deb Burlew

Start cleaning out the White House guest rooms; the illegals are being bused to DC! I hope your neighborhood is flooded with them.

Marah Nimri

Biden go away you did a horrible things to the united state don't do anything more you will destroy everything #trump2024 we need you back

Khalid Khan

Biden what the hell are you support for Russia

Uriel Asimov

Your son is going to prison.too bad the GOOD son died!

Patty Gill

He has to help them they cheated for him he owes them big

Dee Jo

So is our Constitution traitor!

Debbie McHenry

Wow a new service none of us have ever heard of before!

Tammy Wilder-Warner

I have no more words for your useless bs. Your policies prove that we Americans are not your top priority. Maybe illegals with free cell phones, gas cards, etc might think your worth a dime. Your impeachment is coming after mid terms. Documents are drawn up and signatures are ready.

Ghazi Bani Shamsa

Thank you president Donald J. Trump

You are the real president

Lindsay Benoist

Maybe, if you turned the pipeline back on, USPS could afford to deliver mail.

Robert Redditt

A big help, close the border!

Lorinda Case

But not fundamental when they spy on U.S. citizens!

Michael Heaton

The illegals are going to be sent to you in Washington by bus. I hope you can take care of your new voters for the Democrats!? It's very obvious what you're doing the American 🇺🇸 are not stupid. This president is the worst ever it's disgusting.

Kevin Ong

Joe is the real villain

Lori Himes

Impeach this man.. 80 million votes and only 11 million followers... yah he won

John Marron

Exposed the shocking international origins of one bone-chilling attempt to silence a top conservative

The Democrats are summoning their attack dogs.

Anytime a voice on the Right becomes too effective, the Democrat Media Complex gets to work.

But Tucker Carlson exposed the shocking international origins of one bone-chilling attempt to silence a top conservative.

Washington Post writer Taylor Lorenz wrote a deeply dishonest hit piece against a woman who runs a Twitter account called Libs of Tik Tok.

The account simply trawls Tik Tok for videos of insane leftists, many of them educators, publicly confessing their craziness, then puts the content on Twitter.

Libs of Tik Tok allows people to watch deranged leftists express their ideas in their own words, which is why the account is so effective.

The videos aren't deceptively edited or clipped out of context.

The subjects in the videos are so unhinged that any editing tricks could only make them appear less insane than they really are.

And Lorenz, who's reportedly known for doxxing people— attempting to ruin their lives by exposing their personal information online—has now helped do just that to the woman operating the Libs of Tik Tok account.

One of the details in her Washington Post hit piece that went largely unnoticed was the person who actually found out Libs of Tik Tok's identity.

Fox News host Tucker Carlson did a deep dive on Travis Brown, the man behind the doxxing, who allegedly received funding from a foreign government.

"Travis Brown runs the 'Travis Brown Hate Speech Tracker,' which uses a variety of proprietary methods to reveal personally identifying information of private citizens who stray from the approved storyline. Now, who pays for all this? That's the question. Well, the 'Travis Brown Hate Speech Tracker' is funded by something called the Prototype Fund...The prototype fund gets its money not from private donors, but from the government of Germany—Germany's Federal Ministry of Education. It says so right on the website. In other words, what happened to the woman who runs Libs of TikTok, her life being destroyed, was not the work of Taylor Lorenz, the fearless journalist who cries on TV from her PTSD. No, it was a foreign intelligence operation designed to silence and intimidate an American citizen. Wait, is that legal?"

Democrats are hyper-vigilant about any funding coming from foreign sources, yet they're mum on this leftist activist doxxing people.

Brown also happens to be a former Twitter employee.

This is another reason the Left doesn't want Elon Musk to buy Twitter.

The leftist globalist elites view Twitter as their turf. And if conservative stories aren't censored on platforms like it, they know the Democrat Party could be toast and their whole house of cards could fall.

There's no telling how deep the rot goes.

The connections between Big Tech and establishment power brokers must be profound.

Thomas Brown

Has your cognitive deficiency advanced to the point that that you don't even recognize you're not all there?

Casey Brennan

150 global transactions flagged for wrongdoing. All found on the laptop. Get your popcorn ready, the ship is sinking.

Heidy Arguelles

We support #secondamendment

Michael Bee

Fixing elections one step at a time , wanna bet on when the next Covid outbreak will be ?

---}

Joe Biden

April 23rd·

Through the Bipartisan Infrastructure Law, we're investing $25 billion to upgrade and modernize American airports.

(Ok, let's see what Republicans have to say about simply wanting to repair our outdated airports.)

Kevin Johnston

Should have let the airlines go into bankruptcy during the pandemic, now they are raping the people who bailed them out.

Kathryn Sytsma

At tax payers expense

Bill Lauer

How about Inflation

Gerardo Zavala

If your build back better plan is just like your first year in office We the great majority of American people don't want it !!!

LETS GO BRANDON all the way !!!!

Sherry Holland

How about doing something NOW to help with inflation!!!!! I don't care about electric cars that I can't afford I'm worried about paying bills and being able to buy food. Come on November,,worst president ever !!!!!!!!!!

Kristine K.

You need to go Joe. We need to make America great again.

Wade O. W.

Don't airports serve the RICH ?

Frank T. Jr.

Worst president ever. #FJB

Virgil W.

Why is liberal success always measured in the amount of my money your spending to facilitate support of your special interests......

Barbara L.

The people have had enough! Children are hurting, families are hurting and our president could care less! WTH kind of person is he???? Who lets the people suffer like this? Democrats won't honor their oath of office they should be tried for treason and removed

(what do you think Barbara thought about Trump's bungling of covid?)

Steven M.

Today is Saturday, April 23/ 2022 & Joe Biden is the worst President America has ever had.

Deb B.

Joe, the blunderer! In the latest White House gaffe, Biden refers the NHL commissioner as "Batman.

(The guy's name is Gary Bruce Bettmen...Bruce Wayne...Bruce Batman...I can see why Biden might have slipped up here...kinda funny really....How many stupid things did Trump say that this guy lost his mind about?)

Neil B.

The LAST thing this country needs is money wasted on airports. How about making our border secure. How about giving our homeless homes and jobs. How about paying off some cancer medical bills.

Bobbie H.

All I hear is money, money ,money as a tax payer I'm done with the reckless spending!! I can't afford to live but you send 600 of my tax money every week to Ukraine!

Wade O. W.

we are already paying for infrastructure

the bridges in the bay area are $7.

The golden gate is MORE.

This infrastructure spending is just corruption money for his friends and family's secret bank accounts.

Chuck S.

Need the wall finished at boarder. Need bridges fixed and roads.

Jeff B.

So you're basically spending another $25 billion of money we don't have that is printed out of thin air? How is that an "investment" again? You keep using that word. I do not think it means what you think it means.

Jeanine V.

Stop printing money. You are turning us into Venezuela. It won't hurt you or your minions but it sure will hurt We The People.

Joe S.

Yes. That is exactly what is on the minds of every working family American.

You are so disconnected I actually find it amusing. You are done.

Vicki H.

And cause more inflation

(You think she really cares about inflation....does any Republican?)

Wayne W.

Worst investment yet

Tina T.

The heck you are!!! It's all going to Ukraine and in your pockets!!!!¡

Man L. B. R.

You are going to have nicer airports but you will be taxed into poverty. You're welcome America.

Laurie G.

You are always saying you want to help the poor and the middle class do you think they really use the airports they can't even afford to eat

Flower A.

Putin shall win the westerns.

Norbert O.

Fix the border first, you inept over cooked vegetable

Jason H.

Every decision that your admin. makes is the wrong one

Kimberly C.

The best airport upgrade was getting rid of the mask mandates.... but you had nothing to do with that.

(Other than taking covid serious which led to mask mandates being removed...unlike Trump.)

Roxanne C.

Kinda sounds like tax payers paying for a new Buffalo stadium. That actually won't even be in Buffalo.

Gregory S.

Spending your way into more inflation to further cripple Americans.

Our grandchildren will be paying the price for your stupidity. Oh I forgot Joe Biden is not really runny things. Who is really doing this? Ideas ????

Todd N. B. H.

Step aside sippy cup joe let a real president do it.

Cody B.

Cool airports get upgrades, but lower class families don't. People over airports

Andy G.

How about the border

(Lives in Tennessee.)

Dave C.

What an incredible deal...... that's less than half the cost of rearming the taliban.

Maria W.

Take your ball and go home

Jacob H.

Cool. Good idea Joe. NOT!

Pat L.

How will you replace pilots and attendants forced to retire because of your covid mandates ?

Shawn M.

Inflation at its finest

Daryl H.

All talk....just a bunch of mumbo jumbo

(Guess he never heard a Trump speech.)

Cathy D.

Easter Bunny needs to direct you to the border.

(She lives in Oregon...what border is she talking about...Has she ever been there?)

Elanga D.

How many Times did Jesus Christ wash His boday Joe Biden

(What the fuck?)

Gretchen P.

How's the upcoming food shortage issue looking?

(The one that hasn't started? No idea.)

Bama B.

Better idea: finish the wall and end the invasion at the southern border.

Sue H.

Increasing debt rather than cutting and using those funds... Vote buying apparently

Howard S.

Yet airports are so screwed up due to unionized workers for TSA that are feel good useless tools. They miss guns all the time during tests. Time to privatize security where people can actually be fired for doing a bad job. Oh and thanks for mega inflation Jimmy Biden - aka Carter.

Jeanie Q. C.

Follow the law and secure the border! Open borders were tried in other countries and they had street mugging and rapes!

 David W.

OF COURSE WITH INFLATION ALMOST 10% NO ONE CAN AFFORD TO GO ANYWHERE. BIDEN INFLATION. NOT PUTIN...

 Ann S.

Impeach incompetent corrupt puppet Joe

 Jim D.

You have more than that to the Taliban...what about us Americans Joe???

 Theresa N.

BLAH blah blan. The Democrat ain't your Father's Democrat Party. Once the party of the working man is now a party of dictators liars multimillionaires WHITE. Your party left us or began to the day the Kenyan became President. And now he is finishing what he started using you the puppet.

(This genius took a speech by Biden about the Republican party and tried to use it as her own. Aren't they a clever lot... Note the blatant racism at the end. True Trump freak.)

Lori H. A.

Everyone call your governors demand 25 removal of biden and his administration. Before he presses the button

Mike J.

Your a joke old man.

(This guy was 56 years old....not a spring chicken himself.)

Tater Bucket

Actually we're investing $25 billion to line drug dealin' Hunter's pockets. Worst administration in the history of the USA. Wear the badge proud Joe. Let's go Brandon!!!

(Do you believe a guy named Tater Bucket knows what's really going on? I have my doubts.)

Elliott B.

At least under Trump infrastructure week never cost us a dime

(Because Trump never did anything about it.)

Cheryl E.

Biden tried to be popular and unifying — and is neither. His failings discredit his political approach — and it's the same one that has dominated the Democratic Party for decades.

(You really think Trumpers were ever going to give anything Biden did a chance?)

Sam R.

Good one! I bet it will never get done until a Republican steps in.

Brandon D.

Spending future tax dollars and burying us in debt is NOT an investment

Linda M.

Bishop Evans LIFE MATTERED AND YOU JOE BIDEN ARE RESPONSIBLE FOR HIS DEATH......

Brian F.

NOT really a priority right now Brandon

Bill H.

Yep,just like obama's infrastructure joke! Money disappears, nothing got done! Corrupt union bosses were very happy, bankrupt solar company CEOs we're happy and democrat's rich friends were happy! biden learnt something from bama.

Ray J.

Please Joe, give us at least ONE truth during your presidency.

(How many times did Trump lie while in office…30thousand…that we know of.)

Jim P.

So, your ridiculous policies has cost the United States another brave warrior at the Texas border. Doesn't that make your body count 14? That doesn't include the loss of life due to the unrestricted smuggling of fentanyl. Since you no longer have a sufficient amount of cognitive ability, does that allow you to sleep comfortably at night and during your nap time?

Take some time to think long and hard about the legacy you will leave when you have to account for your life.

Jeff D.

After a year, Joe Biden is 'divisive, angry, out-of-touch and dishonest'. I agree but also add incompetent.

Eric R.

Joe shows how much you care about Americans. You give 800 billion to a third world country and you give 25 billion to America's infrastructure nice job Joe

 ***(Whew…that's enough. Apparently repairing airports pisses these people off to.)**

--}

 Joe Biden

"Ensuring worker safety is a national priority and a moral imperative.

On Workers Memorial Day, we honor and remember those who lost their lives on the job and reaffirm every worker's basic right to a safe and healthy workplace."

*(Well, this one is as innocent as they get. Mr. Biden just wants people to be safe on the job. No way Republicans will have anything negative to say about this…right?)

Vijaykumar H

Safety of the southern border is also a nation's priority.

(Not even an American.)

Joan M. O.

… what are you actually doing to ensure worker safety ?

Matthews G.

The future of America is Republican

(Fake account…from Kenya.)

Janine M.

Are you going to honor the National Guard that we lost?

Michael T.

The border should be a priority. And NOT giving college debt *forgiveness. We all paid our debt, now it's their turn.*

 Roxanne O. G.

Real gross domestic product (GDP) decreased at an annual rate of 1.4 percent in the first quarter of 2022. I'm sure this will help workers, NOT. Worst President in modern times.

Roger H.

Except the national guard! You on your own!

?

Trump the best

Make America stronger

(From Egypt.)

Cashmeout A.

WORST president in usa history by far!

(You think Cash me out knows what he is talking about…I don't.)

Josh P.

Nice try but we've already had OSHA for years. Go ahead and take your nap now.

Michael M.

Nothing about our troops that have given their life's for our freedom. Seriously 46?

(Wrong holiday, genius.)

Dee Dee C.

How about forgive cancer debt they didn't ask for it or sign for it!!!!!!!!!!!!!

Baqir Al S.

Trump remains to be the best president ever lead America.

(From Egypt.)

Patrick A. P.

RESPECT PUTIN AND EVERYTHING WILL FALL INTO PLACE.

Russia behaves the way it behaves because since at least 2000 it has been threatened and harassed by the Masonic West. From 2000 to 2015 the U.S. NED has financed with billions of dollars a subversion in Russia to destabilize Putin. Since it did not work because Putin is too popular in his country, The same U.S. NED has financed with five billion dollars a subversion in Ukraine to remove the Yanukovych regime and place a regime vassal of the Masonic West. Then the accord the Masons made with Russia where the reunification of

Germany was obtained against no NATO in Ukraine was trampled underfoot and Masons did all they could to get Putin to foul out. I say to the Masons: stop your criminal game which will only bring about WW3 and nuclear this time. Instead of behaving in such a detestable way the Masonic West must respect Putin and respect Russia the same way the West wants to be respected and everything will fall in place. This is not Putin the criminal but the masons who have imagined this scheming to ultimately place their pawn, Navalny the Mason, at the head of Russia and through him control Russia. Masons deserve to be sent to Guantanamo because they behave like true terrorists.

(The crazy runs deep with this one.)

James G.

Your new Misinformation Governance Board (Ministry of Truth) just wondering when do the armbands come out and what the design will be.

Debbie E. P.

Does a safe and healthy workplace for every worker include those working to secure the southern border Joe? I bet Bishop Evans would have appreciated that. But your border policies make working conditions deadly.

Brandon D.

I think we are all kinda ready to hear a full statement from you on what you know about Hunter and his overseas deals...

Kelly L P.

How many of you people on here can't wait to start paying for everybody's College even all the little rich kids when the Democrats forgive it so they get voters keep that in mind think your taxes are going to go up when that happens

Kimberly A.

You made your momma proud Joe. ..SMH

Jake H.

This is the worst president of all time

Marcia B.

This site of yours is just ONE HUGE LIE..TRUTH IS NOT YOUR FORTE!!!!! BUT LIES ARE!

Mike M.

It's impossible with a clown like Biden trying to destroy America...

Kurt R.

We already have Labor Day, Sniffy. Only you can screw up national holidays.

Robin K.

A Disinformation Governance Board? Are you serious? Your entire administration is disinformation. You lie constantly about everything. No one takes you seriously. By the way, this so-called WMD is a farce.

Sharon S.

How about safety at the southern border you will be remembered the worst president in history and hopefully Hunter goes to jail

(Enraged Trump nut.)

Johnny G.

Possibly the worst father of all time is telling us our children belong to teachers. Hysterical.

(Is this guy serious? Sometimes these Trumpers really are hateful monsters.)

Gil R.

Are you talking about illegal alien invaders coming into our country by the thousands? You need to resign. Every day you distort out country more and more.

(They're so dramatic...The invasion!!! Did they even care before Trump came along? This lady lives in Alabama.)

Marcio S.

This guy works miracles.... woke up the dead from the grave to vote for him.....

(Not a single case of this. Pure Trump crazy.)

Kyle R.

How about you lower the costs of everything back to what they once were? Inflation is crippling us.

Food everywhere is more expensive, haircuts, gas, stores... And don't blame it on Russia. You started this when you illegitimately took office.

We can't afford another two years of Democrats in power.

Danny E.

Reckon those illegals running around all over will help

Angie T.

Joe Biden - lifelong failure. But successful lining his and his family's pockets in shady way

(This lunatic got mad that I laughed at this ridiculous post and went on my page and laughed at every one of my posts till I blocked her...lol.)

Candice M.

The "Disinformation Governance Board" just declared that Sleepy Joe is a fraudulently elected president.

(They get so mad at the idea of having their lies fact checked.)

Crystal H.

What's going on with your daughters diary, Hunters Laptop, biolabs in Ukraine, Epstein flight log, Hillary and the Russian Hoax, the border, the underground tunnels and all the missing children? Oh and the clot shot, fake president and administration.

(Pure Trump conspiracy nut here.)

Coleman M.

You all knew Joe Biden was going to sink the economy but you voted for him anyway. How do you define stupid?

(Curious what exactly these people judge a healthy economy on....gas prices, the stock market, which they, like most of America, have nothing to do with. What exactly is a healthy economy to Coleman...corporations bringing in record gains, unemployment at record lows, equal right for workers....? Who knows.)

Brian Mc

Cool story, so how much are you going to money launder through Ukraine this week? Another couple million? How much are we at now? I guess you've got to repay them for protecting your son HR puffin stuff while getting a little kickback yourself...

Mathew W.

Where's that great unifier bs you promised us to steal the election Joey?

Jimmy C.

#bidencrimefamily

**Nope....even something this innocent enrages them..*

---------------------------------}

Joe Biden

April 22

Thanks to the Bipartisan Infrastructure Law, we're going to plant 1.2 billion trees across the country to begin the vital work of reforesting America. It makes sense and also makes a big difference in our cities and on our city streets.

**(This statement is literally about planting trees...<u>Planting freaking trees!!!!!</u> How can this possibly upset anyone???)*

?

The world is going through a food crisis due to the Ukraine war, due to the damage to agricultural crops, especially wheat. If America took advantage of this deficit and worked to increase the cultivation of food crops, especially wheat, it would be better than trees that have no nutritional value!

Mohammed Y.

Let's go Brandon

Good job joe Biden

(From Saudi Arabia.)

Linda S. O.

All these so called nice comments to crazy Joe must be all the illegals that he let in, cause nobody in their right mind could approve of the way he is handling this country!

Bonnie C. H.

Go to the border deal with the crisis that are unsafe for our USA.

Frank M.

great so when more go homeless, there can be some comfort under them

Cindy J. K.

why don't you work on the real problems facing America? Like the crime problem, the open border, homelessness, and helping seniors who are struggling with high inflation die to our terrible policies?

Jon B.

Let me get this correct (whoever writes Biden post's) over 220,000 immigrants entered our country illegally not to mention get always. The deadly impact of fentanyl that is coming across our borders and you are talking about planting trees?? By the way not your money. So whoever is writing these posts, I don't know how you sleep at night? This is the only employee in the country who has the worse job evaluation and continues to take a vacation and ignore his employer? The rest of us would lose our jobs.

Barbara L.

Destroying America every single way they can. Hope you're all very pleased with this destructive administration.

Susan G.

You're more concerned about climate than protecting our borders the American people prices at the pump inflation. Such a disgrace. Sock puppet!

(I actually think saving the planet is slightly more important than gas prices...but whatever.)

Janie M.

American tax payers are funding the war! ENOUGH IS ENOUGH!!! Over 3Billion dollars given to Ukraine in 2 months. American citizens need to protest against giving so much money to Ukraine to start and, instead, helping the American consumer. Stop raising taxes, gasoline tax, electric and gas taxes, and food prices!!! Americans need more help than Europeans!!!

Ralph S.

gonna make a "big difference" in the National Debt too. Smdh

Edward H. T.

We're broke and you want to plant trees. How about if you start cutting taxes and spending and reducing inflation by getting the Federal reserve to at least aim for a soft landing since they created this mess because of you in Congress.

(Broke...yup, we're out of money. You think Edward has any clue?)

Deb B.

Joe, the blunderer! In the latest White House gaffe, Biden refers the NHL commissioner as "Batman."

(This lady was so excited about this that she cut and paste it on multiple posts...as if it somehow proved her point on everything.)

Man Ley B Rant

You will see more trees around but increased taxes and inflation will have you starving.

(Somehow I just can't take man ley very serious.)

Rachel D.

Please stop claiming that you helping the people that deserve it , you are destroying their businesses , inflation, it's all a lie .

Bobbie H.

Plant trees?? Yet my state in Missouri is seeing all the illegal immigrants shopping with my tax money, and a free phone, yet they have more food in their cart than I do to feed my family

Terry S.

How stupid is this? Close the darn border and send Zelensky what he needs now. It's as if you have NO MIND or sense or REAL morality at all. God help all of us!

(Close the border...as if Biden can just go hang a sign or something...and I guess he missed the part where we are already arming Ukraine.)

Gregory S.

I do not know who is posting for Joe Biden.

I am positive it's not Joe himself just like he is not really running the presidency.

Does anyone have ideas on who this could be? I do and would love to see other's ideas.

Poor frail Joe Biden who is obviously in cognitive decline.

His wife should be ashamed for allowing this elder abuse to continue.

(Another Trump nut.)

Delane John

How embarrassing you are to our country

Mike Pickens

This make no sense, the government uses dozers to clear trees out to build roads and now they going to plant them back ?? Biden son hunter must have bought a tree farm

Vi N.

Joe, can we move US Navy back to the Black Sea and open a huge Okinawa style military base in Romania? I am asking for a friend.

Love Rules

You have caused one crisis after another, how about correcting one crisis at a time instead of piling them up, and up.

(Not gonna take someone named Love Rules too serious, especially when Love is spreading division.)

Samantha K.

Yes .. everyone is concerned with making this happen

Holly M.

Are you going to make a statement about the Texas border soldier who died while saving the life of 2 immigrants>

Theodore S.

So that why you opened up the border and let millions of people in our country to plant trees

Way to go Brandon

(what really needs said about this? Like Biden went down and opened a gate or something.)

Chris H.

I thought we where going to fix the roads and bridges?

Tom B.

Yeah that will help our economy

Chris C.

Worst President Even.

The Red Wave is Coming. 🌊🌊

Debi O. C.

Fix the border.

Hon A. M.

Why not to relocate into bushes instead of planting 1.2 billion dollars into your pocket

Beverly P.

We have tons of trees stupid people

(Can you just see this woman in her small house, never going outside...clueless.)

Rex N.

Maybe the park service needs to stop cutting them down

David W.

These programs will be ripened with fraud.

Heath S.

You couldn't have planted food! You people who worship the earth are going to be be the death of mankind!

(You people who worship the Earth will be the death of mankind…yes, you just read that right. Can you imagine the crazy hate in this guy's heart?)

Rob V. G.

Sidenote, re: the growing anti-democratic voices growing in this country. Bill Maher's closing monologue on Real Time this week may be the most important oped of the century. It should go viral. Before it's all gone: before Nazi bundists take the nation and turn it into the opposite of what it was conceived to be.

Gennan C. C.

Nice trees do not make up for pot-holed, third world streets, Clown Joe.

Andy Green

If you lowered inflation people could actually afford to buy trees

Curt A.

Is that the 2,700 page bill you said you wrote with your own paw the other day?

Doyle A.

Nothing like appeasing old hippies...

(Jesus....what can even be said?)

Keith N. K. R.

Why do you make promises on what you know you won't do

Howard S,

Yet another role NOT for government - thanks for spending more tax dollars that you should not be spending --- thanks for inflation Jimmy Biden.

Mike M.

Let's go Brandon. Biden has destroyed our country in a little over a year

Will G.

Let's go Brandon

Frank F.

So ur gonna steal the money that means

John S.

federal tree planting on a state level issue, concerning planting across the county. What lies do you have left Joe

Mick C.

Which one of your donors was awarded that contract?

Bob J.

Taxpayers are worried if they can cover the bills for the month and democrats are spending money like it grows on trees

Eric S.

Stop SECRETLY using me, or using me in any way, that's MY LIFE ENERGY their using TO HEAL, that VIOLATES MY RIGHTS, and BREAKS DIVINE LAWS.

Barbara O.

Will they start to trim & remove all the underbrush to help prevent fires as well? I read articles that multiple fires in Calif were due to the old Powerline

Poles etc.that were approx 100 yrs old that sparked fires.

Anthony B. K.

More fuel for wildfires in poorly maintained government forests

(Like when Trump suggested forests be raked...?)

Tina M. D.

I see the basement dummy did his creepy whispering again today.

Adam D.

Yeah, because trees are going to help the economy your administration is destroying.

Lorraine C.

What the hell is happening to the food processing plants in this country? I just heard that 21 have either burnt down or have been dismantled. There is now a bird flu epidemic across the country where hundreds of thousands of bird have been killed off due to this flu. Also China has bought thousands of acres of farm land in this country. What the hell are democrats doing to us?

(Good luck with this one. A whole bunch of he said, she said, Trump style bullshit.)

Kilzer SD

Let's Go Brandon! Joe Biden Agrees!

John S.

Eight trillion dollars. That's how much President Joe Biden has proposed in new spending — in just the 2½ months since taking office. It's an absurd figure, equal to more than a third of America's entire yearly economic output.

And it's overwhelmingly meant to transform the nation — to empower and enrich Democratic special interests, lock in permanent Democratic control and impose radical left-wing ideas.

Biden's latest hit: $1.52 trillion in discretionary spending. That follows $1.9 trillion for last month's American Rescue Plan, $2.3 trillion for Part I of his infrastructure plan and another $2 trillion or so expected soon for Part II.

That mind-blowing $7.7 trillion total doesn't even count another $3 trillion or so in entitlement spending and $300 billion in debt-service costs; add that in, and you're talking about spending that's more than half the nation's $21 trillion output.

Norberto F.

Worst president of our time.

Christina S.

So your more worried about planting trees when you have starving elderly people and our vets and homeless living on the street

 Tasha M.

Is that why you are gonna start selling oil permits again? Because you think planting trees is going to have an effect on how much oil they spill.

 John S.

BIDENS CARBON FOOTPRINT, At the heart of the whopping carbon footprint, is the President's fleet of aircraft including a modified Boeing 747 plane known as Air Force One.

According to a report in the Daily Mail, the five planes alone will be responsible for releasing some 2.16 million pounds of carbon dioxide (CO2).

As a security measure, the fleet consists of a decoy as well as C-17 Globemasters - military transport aircraft designed to carry the presidential motorcade and helicopters.

The remainder of President Biden's greenhouse emissions will be emitted by his motorcade, including the armoured presidential Cadillac limousine known as 'The Beast'. The 20,000-pound vehicle belches out an estimated 8.75 pounds of carbon per mile.

For comparison, figures published by the US Environmental Protection Agency show the average car releases 0.89 pounds of CO2 per mile.

President Biden's long motorcade in Italy was attributed to the country's Covid rules, which place restrictions on the number of non-cohabiting people allowed to travel in a single vehicle.

John S.

Close the borders

(Should he go hang a sign?)

Juan D.

Let's Go, Brandon!!! u□□□

Charlene W.

And your contribution to Earth Day was to pollute your way to Seattle and back with a speech you could have delivered from the WH lawn, such a hypocrite. BTW, the tree planting was already rolling under Trump after we joined the Trillion Trees Initiative.

Tricia W.

I keep hearing them say BIDEN the blood is on your hands for all this illegals pouring into this Country. How about this The search for a missing Texas National Guard soldier who went missing Friday while attempting to rescue migrants in a river has been called off for the night.

Johnny K.

Great! While you're at it why don't you dig a big hole next to one of those trees, jump in, and then have a bulldozer bury you in it? As full of crap as you are I'm sure the tree would appreciate the fertilizer.

Jack L.

A balloon is smarter than this chode

Jerry L. P.

November won't get here fast enough.

Clive B.

Is it not time to head to your comfy chair for your afternoon nap yet?

Donald C. C. B.

Quit living in the past. Pass a crime bill

Bobby L.

Do you think you are so low in the polls because you are representing Americans? Are you daft?

(Trump was right around 39% in the polls and still got 70 million plus votes...but polls didn't matter then.)

Stacey N.

So while people are starving and can't pay for gas and afford anything for that matter we can all rest better knowing that Joe Biden is filling out our tax dollars to the Ukraine and to help people plant trees that I'm sure we're never going to see

Patty R.

WHAT ABOUT THE BORDER!

WHAT ABOUT DEPENDING ON OUR OWN RESOURCES FOR FUEL?

PLEASE, PLEASE PEOPLE, DON'T VOTE DEMOCRATIC. THIS ADMINISTRATION IS RUINING MY COUNTRY!

BIDEN DOESN'T GIVE A RAT'S ABOUT AMERICANS!

WAKE UP!

ZZGO BRANDONZZ

Lorisa C.

You all know that is Obama talking right!

Marty M.

This country is the worst it's been since the Carter admin, and you're going to plant trees.....

Danny E.

Another dead GI for adding to the 13.

(Can you imagine people like this in WW1, WW2...we would be speaking German if they were running things.)

Debra B.

You're canceling Title 42? Haven't you ruined enough in your short time in office. You are a complete whack job.

Dany B.

Who actually believes joe biden even knows how to get on face book must less even read the comments his servents type for him to so call say lmao

Jason K. J.

Any word on when The next Trump Rally will be

(Just follow the sheep in red hats.)

Ronnie W.

Biden's approval is lower than disapproval in 40 states, compared to last year when the numbers for the first few months of his presidency showed only 17 states where disapproval outranked approval – and two states where it was tied at zero either way. GET READY FOR THE RED WAVE!!!!!!!!!!!!!!!!!!!!!!!!!

Ellery K.

How many Democrats does it take to change a light bulb? One to change the bulb, six to talk about how wonderful it's going to be when the new bulb is screwed in, and ten to argue for increased funding for solar lighting research.

Greg E.

Thanks to you we have 300,000 get aways so far this year into this country murdering innocent humans, by letting them in

Dan D.

You're killing the country. Idiotic woke/green baloney.

*(Nope...even trees piss these people off. Can you feel the hate?)

------------------------------------}

Joe Biden ·

I grew up in a family where, when prices went up for things like gasoline, it became a discussion at the kitchen table. We felt it.

That's why I'm focused on doing everything I can to lower the cost of gas and energy and accelerate our transition to clean energy.

 **(Ok, so this is a little post about family, something Republicans claim to hold dear, and a pledge to do what he can to help bring down the cost of gas and help usher in clean energy. What could possibly be wrong with this????)*

Joe K.

Putin and his price hike. Definitely the reason that milk, eggs, bread, diapers, formula, and basically everything else a household needs went up. Couldn't possibly be poor policies.

Chloe A.

You need to lower it now! The average American can't even enjoy an

average life. I'm starting to think trump was doing a better job now and I hated him!

(I actually checked this one because it sounded so strange to me...fake account.)

Patricia H.

This is all on you Joe!! Bad decision you have made has caused this.

Andy S.

Well....diesnt seem like it's working ..you tapped into our reserve to lower prices for a week and rugjt back up again...Thanks.. Great job

Scott B.

Leave office. Prices will go back down

James T.

But I thought the president didn't control gas prices....

Muhammad U.

Trump was much better than you..... Every time you are just appreciating yourself..... Everyone know how the inflation rate is increasing day by day due to your sanctions on Russia....

William M.

You couldn't focus on a hotdog that has wheels because cotton candy came from outer space▢

Colleen M. C.

Funny how we didn't have ANY of these problems when we had a strong President……unlike yourself.

David L.

I wonder if you realize that the discussion around many dinner tables is how illegitimate you are?

Ron L.

It's over double since you took office. Way before Putin invaded. Good job

Jacqson G.

We must say that we enjoy your comedy whenever you hit the keyboard

WJ O'C.

You know 2 things about lowering prices. Jack and squat and Jack just left.

(So clever...stole line from Army of Darkness.)

Mostafa H.

The highest prices ever good work Joe

Mark H.

You have never even been to a gas station!

(Biden actually has a car collection...so yeah, he has been to a gas station. Curious though, has Trump ever even driven a car?)

Phill O.

Oh, really? You say this just as I see the prices are shooting back up? Can't you at least make your lies less blatant?

Jan S. N.

You are doing everything but making USA energy independent!

Chris P.

I guess the fuel people don't pay you enough???

Tell us all how you are a 20 times over millionaire????

Lorraine C.

FkUJB. The government get a dividend on every barrel of oil pumped. You and yours just raised the cost of permits by 50%. You know that is going to be added to the price at the pumps.

Irene W.

Its YOUR FAULT things r at rock bottom, STOP letting the left tell u what to do and say ,STAND UP FOR THE AMERICAN PEOPLE FIRST IS THE BORDER, STOP LYING ABOUT IT BEING CLOSED, OPEN OUR PIPE LINES and the people may start caring for u again,lower our gas at the pump and our food, u act as $$$$ GROWS ON TREES,I FEEL SO BAD FOR OUR YOUNG CHILDREN GROWING UP NOW IN THIS INVIRMENT

(The crazy Trump rage runs deep here.)

Ray F.

Some of us are focused on getting you out of the White House

Terry G.

The great destroyer of a country..fascist.

Rick A.

You sort of blew that on day one of your presidency

Josh S.

You are focused on lowering the cost of energy....by raising the cost of energy?? Are you dumb? Or do you think we are?

You can like or dislike renewable energy technologies, but they COST MORE!

Ann He.

It's your fault to start with

Jeff M.

Everything...seriously...keystones still shut down, American exploration...still shut down...

#PutinPriceHike is a joke at best...how about #Bidenflation more like it

(These people believe a section of pipeline that was never built needs to be reopeded....seriously.)

Tanya W.

Everything like allowing America to use our own gas? Doesn't that statement sound like we have a socialist President

Kevin S.

Now as your policies drive up prices on goods and services, you have grown rich from "politics" and don't care about the average citizen.

Ernest C.

Maybe we will make better progress now that cons quit bashing Elon.

(These people are so happy about the possibility of Trump being able to lie on Twitter again after Elon purchased it.)

Gary M. M.

Nothing but incoherent ramblings of an old man lost to dementia

Jesse U.

So your gonna turn the pipeline on and resume American drilling good job

(More pipeline craziness.)

Leon S.

Joe Biden How about returning the country independently fuel efficient like the way you found it. What was your kick back in giving Russia a BILLION dollars a day for fuel? Did you funnel it through your son like your other corrupt dealings.

Peggy D.

It's been months!! You should have done something long ago. All these posts your handlers make are just bs false promises. Gas has gone down 1 cent in our area in the past month. Whoop dee friggin do.

Carlton J.

And how much was a gallon of gas in the mid-1900's?

(It's like he almost accidently realized inflation has existed for a very long time here...almost.)

Susie T. N.

His ideas as a Vice President were awful and as President the bad ideas just keep coming. Only as President it's far worse!

Bev S.

Oh..I get it!! Send Ukraine billions.... That will certainly help Americans with our problems!

Havok B.

You did exactly the opposite

Vicki J.

all you do is lie lie lie.... Like being top of class in college.... very shameful in all your actions

Tim L.

Tossing out the BS flag on this one..........Biden cares about ONE thing.........BIDEN !

Kevin H.

Every country has a different word for hypocrisy. In America, the word we use for hypocrisy is liberal.

Kevin 'Twitch' M.

You don't understand basic economics, do you?

You're a Democrat, of course you don't.

(You think Twitch understands economics?)

Dan C.

You're a complete and total failure

Kevin Nye

Do you and Hunter have dinners to discuss when crack prices go up?

***(Just more of the same...blind hate.)**

---}

ON THE FILP SIDE.....

***(Let's see how these same people react to one of his own, (Former Defense Secretary Mark Esper,) coming out and saying Trump wanted to shoot protestors after the shooting of George Floyd in 2020.)**

"Can't you just shoot them? Just shoot them in the legs

or something?" Trump asked, according to an excerpt in Esper's book "A Sacred Oath," Axios reported.

Craig M.

Anything to sell a book, vermin.

Mark R.

Myself right now. I'm more concerned about what the big guy is doing to us.

Joe A.

The lengths libs go to lmao

Sue C.

What an embarrassment CNN is. Tabloid news.

Barbara Z.

OMG - the hate for this man is VERY disturbing

Tea C. J.

Wow, that must be true if it's coming from a disgruntled former employee and from CNN

Tim M.

Let's go Brandon! AND everyone that voted for him!

Arvid E.

Hyperbole to sell a book. Unless you were in the room, its all hearsay.

John H.

Biden should have to keep the thermostats at the White House as low as I need to keep them at my house so that he can get a sense of the damage he is doing to our nation. My cost for home heating oil has increased 226% since Election Day 2020.

Timothy P.

Didn't we all? I'm just wondering is anything this administration is going to touch not blow up in their face? I've heard the expression cheaters never prosper but wow....

Chad J.

This book will sell about as many copies as Jill Bidens new book.

Hosea S.

Propaganda will not save the sunamy that is coming November

Joe F.

A lot of normal people did. Many knew the entire thing was predicated on a lie.

Steve H.

CNN is FAKE NEWS !!

John C.

Have we ever had such a failure as president then we have now ?

Phil L.

Democrats openly encouraged shooting Police Officers.

Sivus B.

But when Ashli Babbitt was ACTUALLY fatally shot by Pelosi's Schutzstaffel while protesting the election fraud that was ok??

George B.

HILARIOPUS HOW THE TRUMP SLAMDER NEVER STOPS. BUT I KEEP SAYSING THIS IS WHAT HAPPENS OUT OF DESPWEATION TO KEEP A LIBERAL IN THE WHITE HOUSE. AMERICA WILL TURN RED AGAIN IN 2024 AND THE MEDIA AND THE LEFT KNOWS IT. TRULY TERRIFYING FOR THEM.

Wisane M.

Okay

No wonder Ashley barbett was shot at the Capitol it was Trump idea right

Fake news

Eric R. T.

So we should accept looting, burning, crime?

Bob H.

The more Biden fails the more cnn thinks attacking trump is the answer. Talk about disinformation. Let's go Brandon

Ashley H.

I would still think that the Hunter Biden laptop was something Russia came up with and is disinformation if I didn't know CNN is fake news. Have to admire them for them getting Joe Biden elected by lying and suppressing information. They are not honest, but yes they are dedicated.

Jp N.

Fake news

Antonio M C.

#Trump2024 #DurhamReport

John W.

Thats better then giving them a crack pipe

Geoff M

Most are thugs and criminals, not a bad idea.

John M.

LMAO! CNN is pathetic!

Sean H.

By protesters they mean violent rioters

Jim D.

Running them over is just as effective

Tim M.

In case you forgot. Three years ago we were experiencing the greatest economy in the history of the world.

Spencer Roe

They were not protesters, they was insurrectionist burning down state and federal buildings attempting to overthrow the government.

Call them what they really are.

Cameron S.

Talk about this information ! No wonder CNN is tanking

Jason R.

More fake news

Benjamin D.

Terrorist not protesters - Great call President Trump

Crazy how fast the racism comes out when they feel they are amongst themselves.

(Ok, so let's see what these people say on another page...considering they think CNN is fake news....)

Via-**Business Insider.**

Frank S.

how ridiculous to even print such nonsense...

Bill A.

If he said that at all, it was likely in jest. Of course to his enemies it's opportunity.

Brian P.

To those who liked this headline, I hope The United States Department of Justice (and the Internal Revenue Revenue——IRS) are closely monitoring you and the other #fascists.

Levi W.

Calm down Business Insider. The presidential election isn't for 2 1/2 years, no need to start your smear campaign already.

Steve C.

"Protesters"

Steve Cruz

"Protesters"

(Hmm, they don't seem to want to hear it...let's try one of their own networks.)

Via-Fox News 21.

John A.

Ohh, another book deal. somebody got paid to lie...again! I'm sure some tard will believe it though.

Lisa A.

That was my suggestion

(OK...That's enough. But just for shits and giggles, let's go to a pro Trump page and see what these people say about their orange messiah.)

Via- Trump for President 2024.

Elizabeth P-C

Get rid of the mob bring back the Best President Trump for ever . We wouldn't be in this Trouble. Mickey

Allen R.

We need you back Donald. Pastor saiD you are as close to Jesus as one can be. You walk in righteousness love the lord our God with all your heart. He said JESUS sent you to bring back Christian values to Americna."

Gigi L.

I don't believe Biden will last as President for three more years. Resign for health reasons. That leaves us Harris. I would be surprised if she stays in as President. She is nervous as a long tailed cat in a room full of rocking chairs when she has to stand before a mic, but she wants to be treated like royalty. If she goes in I think Democrats will impeach her, she is completely incompetent and no one will work for her. The word on the street is that Speaker of the house is next in chain of command, I dunno that true. We desperately need to get control of both chambers of Congress in fall election. THEN the House can toss Nancy out as speaker and hire The Donald as Speaker. Speaker does not have to be a member of Congress. House can hire a man or woman off the street. The entire Democrat Congress will retire if Donald becomes speaker. I would love to see that.

Linda H. P.

Please President Trump we need you NOW

James L.

Go Donald we all need you around the world

Marian T.

We Americans love our President Trump!

Fran T.

If they don't fix 2020, there will be no 2024 .

Bob H.

Keep going President Trump you're doing fantastic

Rose W.

Something needs done now , look what happened in one year, we will be toast. These Democrats and Rinos have really messed up our

country. Help Us Lord!!!!!!

Gloria W. M.

Now everyone can understand why China and Russia did not want trump reelected. Got to have someone with no balls so they can do what they want. And everyone is laughing at our weak leader. Thank the people that voted for the man that belongs in a nursing home. His wife should be ashamed putting him out there.

Paul C. H.

Just stop the rigged elections

Linda T. M.

We need him NOW !!

Hagop B.

Greatest president ever president Trump 🇺🇸🇺🇸

AJ M.

Waiting for your return, Mr. PRESIDENT

Virginia C.

TRUMP IS STILL MY PRESIDENT

Ted M.

Best President ever, for sure...

Anita C. M.

We Need Your help in Washington!! Calling ALL BIKERS! We need you now. They won't allow our trucks . Please send help

Elaine K.

Amen to that.

We need Trump back now.

Trump is going to fix our Country.

Meda K. S.

Trump this world is in a real mess without you now. The people that didn't like you would love you now we only wish you were here this mess would not be the way it is now. We're living on Dangerous Grounds. We need a strong president we need you Trump

Jane K.

Yes! We need President Trump back and our independence as a country back the way he had it! We had the strongest military, the greatest economy lowest gas prices & taxes! He put America 1st and the people 1st! □□

Gina S.

*WAITING FOR THE COME BACK KID MAKING AMERICA GREAT AGAIN .OR EQUIVALENT Wouldn't have $5.00 per gal Gas at Pumps ,This is Socialism at its Best!! Can't Let it Spread Like CANCER...Biden busy Supporting Putin by not Putting Sanctions on Russia Gas/oil! Suppose to Support UKRIAN! Seems HE'S with Putin .But he himself is an Enemy to AMERICANS AMERICA.While all EYES are on UKRIAN Americans Boarders are being Flooded with ENEMIES ! Thank you DIDEN!! Gotta .**VOTE** All out .2022 . Going all Red..and 2024 or America will find herself being ATTACK as UKRIAN is !! America has No Leadership for HER AMERICANS !! Blessing 2022-2024 No Lib DEMS,No None Americans.***VOTE AMERICANS ONLY!! THIS IS AMERICA.. BE A POLL WATCHER... MUST STOP ALL MAIL IN BALLADS..ONLY AMERICANS **VOTE** THIS IS OUR COUNTRY GIVEN BY GOD THE FATHER THE CREATOR OF THIS GREATEST NATION IN THE WORLD !! RED 2022***2024** Time to Stand together AMERICA..For Together we Stand" DIVIDED We Fall as a FREE NATION of PEOPLE..GOD BLESS AMERICA .YOUNG People WAKE UP to Reality!!AMERICA Could be NEXT !! A Country of Mush Mineso that Believe anything Government tells them long as they get Freebies.. Freebies Will take Yor,You're ***FREEDOMS***BY this Anti American Government! **AMERICANS We're.ONE NATION UNDER GOD . Prayers for America. And Each*

Other..Love Not Hate,Don't let the Devil Steal Your JOY. Peace Joy

Wanda G.

Impeach biden....he wasn't really elected, President TRUMP was.

Soussi M. B.

Dear President Trump American people are waiting for you to come back to the White House before the situation gets worst in Ukraine before another war starts another part of the world Please Please you are the only solution we are all Praying for you to come back.

Fouad H.

He will always be my one and only President!! God, I love that man!! God Bless the U.S.A. and God Bless and protect President Trump and his family from all his haters!! We pray for you all the time and we love you!

Susanne T.

We REALLY need his leadership back right now. Biden and his cronies have made a real mess of our country and seem to be working on destroying our world image as well. Tell me again how the election was fair.... PIDGEON PELLETS!! He was illegally shuffled into office and has done more harm to our country and to the American people in 8 the last months that anyone in the last 50 years! So very, very sad!!

CeeJay D.

Many people didn't understand they didn't have to personally like him to vote for him..I don't feel safe with Biden...

Judy S.

Yes we need our great president Trump really Bad!!! Our America is going to hell because of Biden!'n please Lord we need your help to protect us and fix our America!!

Michele B. J.

If President Trump was in charge this would have never happened ! Putin was afraid of him , but he's not afraid of Biden !

Delia C.

I don't know how he can be able taken the WH? Possibly the ends of this years!! I hopefully will be sooner than we expected! We're so worried about this situation Mr Trump. You try the best to get the WH ! 🙏🙏

Jeannine L.

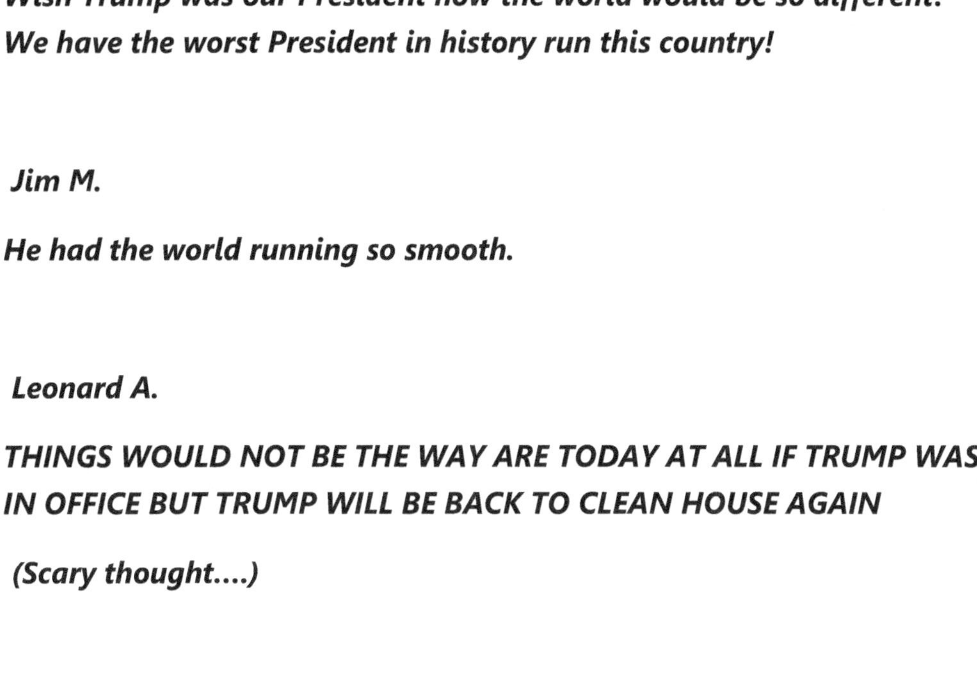

Wish Trump was our President now the world would be so different! We have the worst President in history run this country!

Jim M.

He had the world running so smooth.

Leonard A.

THINGS WOULD NOT BE THE WAY ARE TODAY AT ALL IF TRUMP WAS IN OFFICE BUT TRUMP WILL BE BACK TO CLEAN HOUSE AGAIN

(Scary thought....)

---}

Ok....now, before I go, let's see some of Trump's own tweets. Let's see exactly who these people are so desperate for...who their messiah is.

Trump-Via Twitter.

Hurricane is good luck for Obama again- he will buy the election by handing out billions of dollars.

— Donald J. Trump (@realDonaldTrump) October 30, 2012

It's freezing and snowing in New York—we need global warming!

— Donald J. Trump (@realDonaldTrump) November 7, 2012

The concept of global warming was created by and for the Chinese in order to make U.S. manufacturing non-competitive.

— Donald J. Trump (@realDonaldTrump) November 6, 2012

.@cher—I don't wear a "rug"—it's mine. And I promise not to talk about your massive plastic surgeries that didn't work.

— Donald J. Trump (@realDonaldTrump) November 13, 2012

China's Communist Party has now publicly praised Obama's reelection. They have never had it so good. Will own America soon.

— Donald J. Trump (@realDonaldTrump) November 8, 2012

.@ariannahuff is unattractive both inside and out. I fully understand

why her former husband left her for a man- he made a good decision.

— Donald J. Trump (@realDonaldTrump) August 28, 2012

Everyone knows I am right that Robert Pattinson should dump Kristen Stewart. In a couple of years, he will thank me. Be smart, Robert.

— Donald J. Trump (@realDonaldTrump) October 22, 2012

Robert I'm getting a lot of heat for saying you should dump Kristen- but I'm right. If you saw the Miss Universe girls you would reconsider.

— Donald J. Trump (@realDonaldTrump) October 18, 2012

Remember, new "environment friendly" lightbulbs can cause cancer. Be careful— the idiots who came up with this stuff don't care.

— Donald J. Trump (@realDonaldTrump) October 17, 2012

What a convenient mistake: @BarackObama issued a statement for Kwanza but failed to issue one for Christmas. http://t.co/DodG53Rx

— Donald J. Trump (@realDonaldTrump) December 28, 2011

Remember, I said Derek don't sell your Trump World Tower apartment...its been lucky for you. The day after he sold it, he broke his foot.

— Donald J. Trump (@realDonaldTrump) October 17, 2012

After Friday's Twilight release, I hope Robert Pattinson will not be seen in public with Kristen—she will cheat on him again!

— Donald J. Trump (@realDonaldTrump) November 13, 2012

An 'extremely credible source' has called my office and told me that @BarackObama's birth certificate is a fraud.

— Donald J. Trump (@realDonaldTrump) August 6, 2012

I will start reviewing various political reporters etc & websites as to their professionalism & fairness—many people asking for this.

— Donald J. Trump (@realDonaldTrump) November 2, 2012

Why is Obama playing basketball today? That is why our country is in trouble!

— Donald J. Trump (@realDonaldTrump) November 6, 2012

China's Communist Party has now publicly praised Obama's reelection. They have never had it so good. Will own America soon.

— Donald J. Trump (@realDonaldTrump) November 8, 2012

My twitter followers will soon be over 2 million—& all the "biggies." It's like having your own newspaper.

— Donald J. Trump (@realDonaldTrump) October 17, 2012

Wind turbines are not only killing millions of birds, they are killing the finances & environment of many countries & communities.

— Donald J. Trump (@realDonaldTrump) October 17, 2012

.@katyperry is no bargain but I don't like John Mayer—he dates and tells—be careful Katy (just watch!).

— Donald J. Trump (@realDonaldTrump) October 19, 2012

My twitter has become so powerful that I can actually make my enemies tell the truth.

— Donald J. Trump (@realDonaldTrump) October 17, 2012

It's Thursday. How much money did Barack Obama waste today on crony green energy projects?

— Donald J. Trump (@realDonaldTrump) October 18, 2012

The brass in #TRUMP Tower's atrium is polished twice a month like clockwork. I keep the atrium impeccable. Key to its success!

— Donald J. Trump (@realDonaldTrump) October 22, 2012

Just made the point at #NCGOPcon that "we have to protect our border & I think everyone here knows, nobody can build a wall like Trump!"

— Donald J. Trump (@realDonaldTrump) June 7, 2015

While Jon Stewart is a joke, not very bright and totally overrated, some losers and haters will miss him & his dumb clown humor. Too bad!

— Donald J. Trump (@realDonaldTrump) June 1, 2015

I would like to wish everyone, including all haters and losers (of which, sadly, there are many) a truly happy and enjoyable Memorial Day!

— Donald J. Trump (@realDonaldTrump) May 24, 2015

---}

How about some dumb quotes....

1 "We're rounding 'em up in a very humane way, in a very nice way. And they're going to be happy because they want to be legalized. And, by the way, I know it doesn't sound nice. But not everything is nice."

2 "John McCain is not a war hero. He's a war hero - he's a war hero 'because he was captured. I Like people that weren't captured, OK, I hate to tell you."

3 *I could stand on the corner and shoot somebody and would not lose any voters*

4 *"Sorry losers and haters, but my IQ is one of the highest - and you all know it! Please don't feel so stupid or insecure, it's not your fault."*

5 *"Donald J. Trump is calling for a total and complete shutdown of Muslims entering the United States until our country's representatives* can figure out what the hell is going on."

6 "The concept of global warming was created by and for the Chinese in order to make U.S. manufacturing non-competitive."

7 "It's really cold outside, they are calling it a major freeze, weeks ahead of normal. Man, we could use a big fat dose of global warming!"

8 "I think if this country gets any kinder or gentler, it's literally going to cease to exist."

9 "I will build a great, great wall on our southern border, and I will have Mexico pay for that wall. Mark my words."

10 "They're sending people that have lots of problems, and they're bringing those problems with us. They're bringing drugs. They're bringing crime. They're rapists.

And some, I assume, are good people."

11 "[Overseas] we build a school, we build a road, they blow up the school, we build another school, we build another road, they blow them up, we build again. In the meantime we can't get a fucking school in Brooklyn."

12 What I won't do is take in two hundred thousand Syrians who could be ISIS... I have been watching this migration. And I see the people. I mean, they're men. They're mostly men, and they're strong men. These are physically young, strong men. They look like prime-time soldiers. Now it's probably not true, but where are the women?... So, you ask two things. Number one, why aren't they fighting for their country? And number two, I don't want these people coming over here."

13 To be blunt, people would vote

for me. They just would. Why? Maybe because I'm so good looking."

14 "North Korean Leader Kim Jong Un just stated that the "Nuclear Button is on his desk at all times." Will someone from his depleted and food starved regime please inform him that I too have a Nuclear Button, but it is a much bigger & more powerful one than his, and my Button works!"15

15 *[Kim Jong-Un] speaks and his people sit up at attention. I want my people to do the same.*

16 *"I'm intelligent. Some people would say I'm very, very, very intelligent."*

17 *The concept of shaking hands is absolutely terrible, and statistically I've been proven right."*

18 *"We're gonna build a wall, and*

we're gonna make the Mexicans pay for it!"

19 "There was no collusion!

20. ""They talk about cases, and the cases are created because of the fact that we do tremendous testing."

--------------------------------}

The End...... *God*

Willing.

Remember.

"And we fight. We fight like hell. And if you don't fight like hell, you're not going to have a country anymore,"

Trump Jan-6th. Part of the insanity that sparked the Capital building riot.

John McCain

<u>John McCain</u>...*Let us never forget what Trump said about him either....*

"He was a war hero because he was captured. I like people who weren't captured."

**Fact- I leave you with this sobering fact. No matter who you are, no matter where you live, the dumbest person you know...is a Trump supporter. It's a fact of life we all share....you know it's true.*

Should that person...and his or her ilk be put in charge...of anything?????

Trump: 'I Have Done More For Christianity Than Jesus'

In response to the Christianity Today editorial calling for his removal, Trump called the magazine a "left-wing rag" and said, "I have done more for Christianity than Jesus."

"I mean, the name of the magazine is Christianity Today, and who is doing more for Christians today? Not Jesus. He disappeared; no one knows what happened to him. But I'm out there every day protecting churches from crazy liberals."

Other Books By This Author...

Citrus County.

A short book dedicated to the county that I grew up in, Citrus County. What did a little county in the middle of Florida, one without any big-name city, have to offer...well, a lot actually. Take a trip back in time as I describe Citrus County...the way it once was...the way it is now, it may just bring back a few memories of your own...no matter what little town you yourself grew up in. At the very least, you might have a few laughs.

Ybor Nights.

Ybor City. When I was a

kid, as far back as middle school, all I ever heard about was what a wild ride Ybor was. Growing up in the middle of nowhere, the stories I heard, about girls, girls doing amazing things, awful things, fantastic things, were enough to keep me interested...wanting a taste. Years later, when it came time for me and my friends to make our mark...we took on Ybor, and it was everything that we had dreamed of, and nothing at all like what we expected. Those were Ybor's glory days...those were our glory days. This is our story.

www.ingramcontent.com/pod-product-compliance
Lightning Source LLC
Chambersburg PA
CBHW072300260726

48658CB00004BA/1325